APOSTLE DAVID A. DAVIS

POWER

P OF

PRAYER

PRACTICAL KEYS FOR
POWERFUL PRODUCTIVE PRAYER

ISBN: 978-1505357424

Printed in USA by

Dedication

This book is dedicated to my lovely and anointed wife Pastor Sharon Davis who has been uniquely crafted by God to serve in ministry with me. She is an awesome wife, devoted and inspirational mother, grandmother and effective leader.

To my children (Anthony, Audrey, Latasha and Terrence) who consistently have encouraged me to write. I also dedicate this work to my precious grandchildren Neveah, Michael, Terrell, Jeremiah, Khamiya, and Kerri who fills my life with great joy. I pray to leave behind a legacy of faith for each of you to follow. To the Greater Life Church family who is my crown of rejoicing in the Lord.

To all the Christian leaders, both near and from afar, who have deposited into my life, the spiritual truths and principles that has galvanized my faith and enhanced my love for Christ.

Last, but certainly not least, my Lord and Savior Jesus Christ who I am eternally grateful for His choosing me to be a servant in His wonderful Kingdom.

Contents

Foreword

Apostle David Davis has done an excellent job in creating a working model on effective prayer for the Body of Christ. We need more tools to help believers build lifestyles that are impactful. This book is both a model and tool destined to bless multitudes. All we do as believers should have its origin in the Word of God and be based solely on the Word of God.

I especially appreciate how Apostle Davis highlights principles, provides purpose and reveals distinctive practices necessary for the believer to advance in prayer. Apostles have a burden for the advancement of the Kingdom of God. The Lord tells us to pray for the Kingdom to come and for His will to be done in the earth as it is in heaven. The development of the believer's life in prayer is a critical part for this to the Kingdom manifesting and advancing in the earth.

I recommend this book and I commend Apostle Davis for the consistency he has demonstrated over the years with his weekly prayer line and annual prayer gathering. May the pages of this book refresh and inspire you in the place of prayer.

- Apostle Stephen A. Garner, Senior Leader, Rivers of Living Water Ministries International
Founder of Global Strategic Alliance
Noted author of over 20 published books and ministry training manuals

This manual is absolutely a work from a Kingdom servant that operates "intimately and instructionally" in prayer. I have witnessed close hand and from afar the prayer life of Apostle David and Pastor Sharon Davis over a twenty year period. Dr. Davis has definitely blessed the Body of Christ with a tool that will enhance believers to overcome one of the hardest things about prayer, praying.

This manual will stir the seeker in every believer by providing quick Scriptural reference concerning the heart of God and the prayers we direct to Him. Who else, but a man who knows God, would boldly tell us that our prayers "releases God to get involved in human affairs"? Dr. Davis knows that God will involve Himself into our affairs first hand as a petitioner. It is because of his intercession God intervened into my life with salvation power. The Greater Life Church family, founded by Apostle David and Pastor Sharon Davis, has its roots and foundation firmly fixed on the application of the truths concerning prayer found in this hand book.

It is my desire that all who would receive this manual would receive it not casually. I pray that the manual be recognized and used as a supplement and reference to Scripture as well as a tangible piece of Apostle Davis' ministry of prayer. The questions at the end of each chapter allows for the type of reflection needed to become a "doer of the word" concerning prayer. Beloved, join me in thanking God for His servants of prayer, Apostle David and Pastor Sharon Davis by not only reading this manual but praying through and with this manual.

Christopher J Fitzgerald, MS
Pastor, Testimony of Jesus Ministries

Preface

This book is written in the form of a teaching manual so that any church leader or small group leader can use it to equip people in becoming more effective in prayer. These lessons are a compilation of the principles of prayer I have learned throughout my years as a Christian. It is my prayer that these lessons will enlighten and equip the believer to become more fervent, faithful and fruitful in the spiritual discipline of prayer.

Introduction

The purpose of this prayer manual is to serve as an equipping tool for believers. It is my desire to be a resource for the Body of Christ to help upgrade the believer to pray more effectively and get results! Our Heavenly Father's desire is that His church would be a house of prayer for all nations. (Mark 11:17) "And he taught, saying unto them, Is it not written, My house shall be called of all nations the house of prayer? But ye have made it a den of thieves." It has been said that prayer is the engine room of the kingdom. Jesus, said when we pray, say Thy kingdom come, Thy will be done (Matthew 6:10). Prayer is how God's kingdom and His will is revealed and established in the earth realm.

Prayer is both intimate and instructional. It's intimate because it is an intentional, intimate, heart to heart interaction with our Heavenly Father, which yields the exchange of His nature for ours. As we interact with the Father by the means of prayer, we become more like Him. The Rulers in the Book of Acts recognized that the boldness of Peter and John was a direct result of the intimate time they had spent with Christ. (Acts 4:13) "Now when they saw the boldness of Peter and John, and perceived that they were unlearned and ignorant men, they marveled; and they took knowledge of them, that they had been with Jesus." The more we spend time with the Lord, the more we become like Him.
(2 Corinthians 3:18) validates this, "But we all, with open face beholding as in a glass the glory of the Lord, are changed into the same image from glory to glory, [even] as by the Spirit of the Lord."

Prayer is instructional because of the various principles and strategies we learn from the teaching of Scriptures. Such as praying in the name of Jesus, (John 14:13) "And whatsoever ye shall ask in my name, that will I do, that the Father may be glorified in the Son." Jesus grants us the delegated authority to use His name as a guarantor of answered prayer. Also the power of praying Scripturally, (1 John 5:14-15), And this is the confidence that we have in him, that, if we ask anything according to his will, he heareth us: And if we know that he hears us, whatsoever we ask, we know that we have the petitions that we desired of him.

Power of Prayer

This manual is a compilation of various revelations I learned about prayer. My prayer is that it will bless you to grow more intimately in your fellowship with Christ as well as more effectively in prayer. The Word declares in (James 5:16) that the effectual fervent prayer of the righteous avails much.

Lesson 1
Practicality of Prayer

Confess to one another therefore your faults (your slips, your false steps, your offenses, your sins) and pray [also] for one another, that you may be healed and restored [to a spiritual tone of mind and heart]. The earnest (heartfelt, continued) prayer of a righteous man makes tremendous power available [dynamic in its working]. (James 5:16 AMP)

Introduction: The practice of prayer has a life changing impact. This lesson will help you to understand the purpose, principles and practice that causes the release of power in prayer.

Prayer is an **intentional** encounter with God that builds an **intimate** relationship with the Father and releases Him to get **involved** in human affairs. (Exodus 3:1-8, Hebrews 4:16).

Prayer is an intimate continual dialogue with God, for the purpose of bringing us into partnership and participation with the Lord for the fulfillment of His purpose in the earth.

Prayer is often lopsided; it actually starts with God pursuing us rather than us pursing Him.

"No man can come to me, except the Father which hath sent me draw him: and I will raise him up at the last day." (John 6:44)

"The LORD hath appeared of old unto me, [saying], Yea, I have loved thee with an everlasting love: therefore with loving kindness have I drawn thee."
(Jeremiah 31:3)

God receives extreme pleasure when we commune with Him in prayer. (Proverbs 15:8) "The sacrifice of the wicked [is] an abomination to the LORD: but the prayer of the upright [is] his **_delight_**."

Types of Prayers:
(1 Timothy 2:1) "I exhort therefore, that, first of all, supplications, prayers, intercessions, [and] giving of thanks, be made for all men."

Supplication: (Greek: deēsis or de-a-sis) need, want, a seeking, asking, entreating God for favor.

Prayers: (Greek: proseuchē or pros-yu-kha) earnest prayer manifesting seriousness and sincerity.

Intercessions: (Greek: enteuxis or en-tyu-kses) meeting with, petition, to make attack to reach the mark. To pray on behalf of another.

Giving of thanks or thanksgiving: (Greek: eucharistia) expression of gratitude or appreciation to God for who He is and what He has done.

We are mandated to Pray: (Jeremiah 33:3, 1 Timothy 2:1-4).
(Luke 18:1) "And he spake a parable unto them [to this end], that men ought always to pray, and not to faint;" **_"Prayerful people are powerful people!"_**

Prayer shows that we are truly depended upon God. You can't mature without it. (Psalms 65:2) "O thou that hearest prayer, unto thee shall all flesh come."

Hindrances to effective prayer:
Self- Matthew 26:41
Sin- Psalm 66:18, Jeremiah 5:25
Strife- 1 Peter 3:7
Scriptural ignorance- James 4:3
Satan- Daniel 10:12-13

Helps to effective prayer:

Jesus's name gives us authority- John 16:23

Word of God gives us authenticity- 1 John 5:14-15

Faith gives us activity- Mark 11:24

Praise gives us advancement - Acts 16:25-26

Holy Spirit gives us anointing - Romans 8:26

Partnership with other Believers gives us agreement - Matthew 18:19

Prayer Produces:

Relationship- James 4:8

Revelation- Proverbs 3:6

Refreshing- Psalm 16:11

Recovery- Isaiah 38:1-5, 1 Samuel 30:8

Rescue- Acts 16:25-26, Paul and Silas, Acts 12 Peter from prison

Release of miracles- Acts 4:29-33

Regulates the mind- Philippians 4:6-7

Removes mountains- Matthew 21:21

Repels enemies- Exodus 17:9-13

Practicing the Power of Prayer: Use the following Scripture as a means of Prayer, Praise and Prophetically Declaring the Word over your life.

Example: (Psalms 91:15) "He shall call upon me, and I will answer him: I [will be] with him in trouble; I will deliver him, and honor him."

Prayer: Father I pray that when I call upon You, You will answer me and be with me in trouble. Father let me experience Your delivering grace. Allow me to receive the honor that comes from You.

Praise: Father I praise You for answering all of my prays. Thank You for Your presence that comforts and delivers me in all my trouble. I worship You for bestowing Your honor upon me.

Prophetic declaration: I declare that all of my prayers are answered! God's powerful presence is forever with me in trouble. I experience God's miraculous deliverance and the honor of God is upon my life.

Try the Praying, Praising and Prophetic declaration exercise by using the following Scriptures or some Scriptures of your own choosing:

"Bless the Lord, O my soul: and all that is within me, bless his holy name. Bless the Lord, O my soul, and forget not all his benefits: Who forgiveth all thine iniquities; who healeth all thy diseases; Who redeemeth thy life from destruction; who crowneth thee with loving kindness and tender mercies;" (Psalms 103:1-4)

Prayer: _____

_____

_____

Praise: _____

_____

_____

Prophetic Declaration: _____

_____

_____

Questions:

Write down what comes to mind when you think on the definition of prayer:
Prayer is an **intentional** encounter with God that builds an **intimate** relationship with the Father and releases Him to get **involved** in human affairs.

_____

_____

_____

_____

How does knowing the fact that God delights in your prayers motivate you to pray?

_____

_____

_____

_____

What do you believe is your biggest hindrance in praying?

_____

_____

_____

_____

Power of Prayer

Which one of the prayer helps do you need to become effective in? What is your plan on increasing your effective use of this help?

_____

_____

_____

_____

Which one of the results of prayer excites you most and why?

_____

_____

_____

_____

Which result would you like to see more of in your life? What step can you take to make sure that this result becomes a reality in your life?

_____

_____

_____

_____

Lesson 2
Prayer is a Personal Relationship with God

"And Adam knew his wife again; and she bare a son, and called his name Seth: For God, [said she], hath appointed me another seed instead of Abel, whom Cain slew. And to Seth, to him also there was born a son; and he called his name Enos: then began men to call upon the name of the LORD." (Genesis 4:25-26)

After the fall of mankind and the murder of Abel by Cain, God gave Adam and Eve another seed which was Seth. Seth's name meant "appointed, compensation, take one's stand." Seth was the appointed seed of the prophetic promise for the Messiah to come through. Seth's son Enos whose name meant "mankind" understood the only way mankind could be restored was by returning to an intimate and obedient relationship with the Father. "And he called his name Enos: then men began to call upon the name of the Lord.

The Hebrew word "call" in (Genesis 4:26) is "qara" which means to summon, invite, call for, to commission, appoint, endow, proclaim, be named.

In prayer we are to call upon God's holy and sovereign name. His name is a place of safety for the righteous, (Proverbs 18:10) states, "The name of the LORD [is] a strong tower: the righteous runneth into it, and is safe."

We are to proclaim (announce publicly, loudly and clearly) His name.
"And he said, I will make all my goodness pass before thee, and I will proclaim the name of the LORD before thee; and will be gracious to whom I will be gracious, and will shew mercy on whom I will shew mercy." (Exodus 33:19)

Benefits of Calling Upon the Lord:

"For what nation [is there so] great, who [hath] God [so] nigh unto them, as the LORD our God [is] in all [things that] we call upon him [for]?" (Deuteronomy 4:7)

"I will call upon the LORD, [who is worthy] to be praised: *so shall I be saved from mine enemies."* (Psalms 18:3)

"He shall call upon me, and *I will answer him: I [will be] with him in trouble; I will deliver him, and honour him."* (Psalms 91:15)

"Call unto me, and *I will answer thee, and show thee great and mighty things, which thou knowest not."* (Jeremiah 33:3)

A Personal Prayer life results in:
Divine Delight: "The sacrifice of the wicked [is] an abomination to the LORD: but the prayer of the upright [is] his delight." (Proverbs 15:8)

Divine Development: "Now the Lord is that Spirit: and where the Spirit of the Lord [is], there [is] liberty. But we all, with open face beholding as in a glass the glory of the Lord, are changed into the same image from glory to glory, [even] as by the Spirit of the Lord." (2 Corinthians 3:17-18)

Divine Deliverance: "I will call on the LORD, [who is] worthy to be praised: so shall I be saved from mine enemies." (1 Samuel 22:4)

Divine Dump: "Cast all your cares upon Him; for He careth for you."
(1 Peter 5:7)

Divine Download: "Call unto me, and I will answer thee, and show thee great and mighty things, which thou knowest not." (Jeremiah 33:3)

In order for your relationship with God to remain effective, your prayer life must be intimate and consistent. You must spend quality time learning and listening to the voice of God. Always remember what He has to say to us is more important then what we say to Him, His words are spirit and life!
"Neither have I gone back from the commandment of his lips; I have esteemed the words of his mouth more than my necessary [food]." (Job 23:12)

"It is the spirit that quickeneth; the flesh profiteth nothing: the words that I speak unto you, [they] are spirit, and [they] are life." (John 6:63)

Questions:

What aspect of calling upon the Lord do you most appreciate?

_____

_____

_____

_____

How would you rate your personal prayer time with God? On a scale from 1-5? Five being the highest.

1------------------**2**--------------------**3**-------------------**4**--------------------**5**

How can you make your personal prayer time with God of greater quality? Suggestions: more time, Scripture reading, praise or worship music.

_____

_____

_____

_____

Power of Prayer

Spend the next 5 days in prayer on the 5 personal prayer results: Delighting in the Lord, Developing spiritually, seeking deliverance, dumping your cares on God, receiving divinely downloaded wisdom.

Lesson 3
Purity of Prayer

Draw nigh to God, and he will draw nigh to you. Cleanse [your] hands, [ye] sinners; and purify [your] hearts, [ye] double minded. (James 4:8)

It is imperative for us to always remember that a pure heart is paramount to praying effectively and getting the results that God said we can have. We can only draw near to God in confidence, when our hearts are pure.

Pure implies clean and clear. Our hearts must be clean and clear before God so that there is clear transmission for transformation. We ought to ask God daily to search our hearts and help us to remove any and all sinful attitudes and actions from us.

"Search me, O God, and know my heart: try me, and know my thoughts: And see if [there be any] wicked way in me, and lead me in the way everlasting.
(Psalms 139:23)

Lack of purity steals our confidence: "For if our heart condemn us, God is greater than our heart, and knoweth all things." (1 John 3:20)

The enemy would like nothing more than to rob us of our God confidence. He often does this by getting us to sin or harbor ill feelings toward others. He is the accuser of the brethren. *"And I heard a loud voice saying in heaven, Now is come salvation, and strength, and the kingdom of our God, and the power of his Christ: for the accuser of our brethren is cast down, which accused them before our God day and night." (Revelation 12:10)*

Lack of purity gives the enemy ammunition to oppose us: "Then he shewed me Joshua the high priest standing before the angel of the LORD, and Satan standing at his right hand to accuse him. And the LORD said to Satan, "The LORD rebuke you, O Satan! The LORD who has chosen Jerusalem rebuke you! Is not this a brand plucked from the fire?" Now Joshua was standing before the angel, clothed with filthy garments. And the angel said to those who were standing before him, "Remove the filthy garments from him." And to him he said, "Behold, I have taken your iniquity away from you, and I will clothe you with pure vestments." (Zechariah 3:1-4)

Blood of Jesus must be applied to our lives daily to help us remain confident as we go before God in prayer: "How much more shall the blood of Christ, who through the eternal Spirit offered himself without spot to God, purge your conscience from dead works to serve the living God?" (Hebrews 9:14)

"<u>The blood of Christ can purge</u> (clear one of a charge or unwanted feeling, memory or condition) <u>your conscience</u> (inner voice and feelings which guides a person to adhere to a righteous course of life or weigh heavy upon a person with a sense of guilt.)" (Hebrews 9:14)

We must keep our conscience always free from offense towards God and men: "And herein do I exercise myself, to have always a conscience void of offense toward God, and [toward] men." (Acts 24:16)

This can be accomplished by always asking for and receiving forgiveness from God who is rich in mercy. "Who forgives all your iniquity, who heals all your diseases." (Psalms 103:3)

We should also pursue peace with all men: "Work at living in peace with everyone, and work at living a holy life, for those who are not holy will not see the Lord." (Hebrews 12:14 NLT)

A Clean and Clear conscience is the key to bold praying and the assurance of being answered by God: "Let us draw near with a true heart in full assurance of faith, having our hearts sprinkled from an evil conscience, and our bodies washed with pure water." (Hebrews 10:22)

"Who may climb the mountain of the LORD? Who may stand in his holy place? Only those whose hands and hearts are pure, who do not worship idols and never tell lies. They will receive the LORD's blessing and have a right relationship with God their savior." (Psalms 24:3-5)

"Having therefore, brethren, boldness to enter into the holiest by the blood of Jesus," (Hebrews 10:19)

I thank God, whom I serve from [my] forefathers with pure conscience, that without ceasing I have remembrance of thee in my prayers night and day;"
(2 Timothy 1:3)

"Let us therefore come boldly unto the throne of grace, that we may obtain mercy, and find grace to help in time of need." (Hebrews 4:16)

Questions:

What would you say your confidence level is in prayer? On a scale of 1-5, 5 being the highest.

1------------------2--------------------3-------------------4--------------------5

_____

_____

_____

_____

Can you name any personal character flaws in your life that gives the enemy ammunition to accuse you?

_____

_____

_____

_____

Spend some time praying and ask God to purge your conscience from anything that will hinder your confidence in prayer.

Lesson 4
Keys to Effective Partnership Prayer

Corporate partnership prayer is probably one of the most neglected and misunderstood forms of prayer we find described in the Bible. Usually when Christians get together to pray, a whole array of prayers are offered by each individual instead of the group simply bringing a few focused and targeted prayer request in complete unison before the Lord. Corporate prayer is extremely powerful when we truly appreciate its value and perform it correctly.

1) Agenda: Partnership Prayer should be based on God's agenda: God is more committed to His kingdom assignment than our own personal agendas.
(Acts 2:1-3, 4:24-31, 12:5-17, 13:1-4, 14:23, 16:13-16)

And Jesus came and spake unto them, saying, All power is given unto me in heaven and in earth. Go ye therefore, and teach all nations, baptizing them in the name of the Father, and of the Son, and of the Holy Ghost: Teaching them to observe all things whatsoever I have commanded you: and, lo, I am with you always, even unto the end of the world. Amen. (Matthew 28:18-20)

"And this is the confidence - the assurance, the [privilege of] boldness - which we have in Him: [we are sure] **that if we ask anything (make any request) according to His will (in agreement with His own plan) He listens to and hears us**, And if (since) we [positively] know that He listens to us in whatever we ask, we also know [with settled and absolute knowledge] that we have [granted us as our present possessions] the requests made of Him." (1 John 5:14-15 Amp)

2) Agreement: Partnership Prayer should be with agreement. How can two walk together except they be agreed? (Amos 3:3), (Acts 2:1-3, 4:24-31, 12, 13:1-5)
Five times in the first five chapters of Acts, the Bible tells us that the disciples were on "one accord." Each time, it's the Greek word "homothumadon," a compound word that basically means "same passion, combined heat, shared glow, having the same mind, or being in agreement mentally about the same thing. There was among the Apostles a mutual experience of the same burning heart, the same heart passion. This ardor of heart unity, fellowship, and agreement in purpose, desire, attitude and action marked the dynamic nature of their praying together which was instrumental in the release of kingdom power.

Unity was very important to Jesus. In the last moments with His disciples, He prayed earnestly for that oneness. Listen to His heart-cry to the Father, not just for those immediate disciples, but for you and me: "I pray not only for these, but also for those who believe in Me through their message. ***May they all be one, as You, Father, are in Me and I am in You. May they also be one in Us***, *so the world may believe You sent Me.* I have given them the glory You have given Me. May they be one as We are one. I am in them and You are in Me. May they be made completely one, so the world may know You have sent Me and have loved them as You have loved Me." (John 17:20-23)

We reflect God's glory to the lost and hallow God's name through our loving, selfless, servant like attitudes toward one another. This harmony is directly connected to God's manifest presence and power in the pages of Scripture. When we agree or symphonize together in corporate partnership prayer at the same time for the same thing, the power of the Holy Spirit is released in a much greater way, bringing swift breakthroughs and answers to prayer. Towards the end of (Matthew 18:19) we read, "... whatever they shall ask, it will come to pass and be done for them by My Father in heaven." The word "done" is defined by the Strong's Concordance as follows: Strong's #G1096 ginomai - ghin'-om-ahee - means to generate, to become or come into being, to come into existence, begin to be, receive being, be assembled, come to pass, be finished, be fulfilled, be made, ordained to be, be performed, be wrought. The meaning conveyed here strongly suggests something which had not yet taken place will take place. I think it even goes further in that it implies something which had not existed before will come into being or into existence.

3) Anointing: Corporate Prayer releases a more intensified anointing.
[[A Song of degrees of David.]] Behold, how good and how pleasant [it is] for brethren to dwell together in unity! [It is] like the precious ointment upon the head, that ran down upon the beard, [even] Aaron's beard: that went down to the skirts of his garments; As the dew of Hermon, [and as the dew] that descended upon the mountains of Zion: for there the LORD commanded the blessing, [even] life for evermore." (Psalms 133:1-3)

Partnerships manifest our maturity to value the strength of our unity and the dynamic working of God's power through it. It causes the anointing to flow upon each person and releases the commanded blessing upon the corporate man. Like the dew, it causes the favor of God to manifest in ways we can't even imagine.

Dew is something you don't see visibly transpiring but it shows up to refresh and revives living plants. Our unity will cause the invisible yet tangible favor of God to show up in every area of the believer's life.

"And it shall come to pass in that day, that his burden shall be taken away from off thy shoulder, and his yoke from off thy neck, and the yoke shall be destroyed because of the anointing." (Isaiah 10:27)

"The Spirit of the Lord is upon Me, because He hath anointed Me to preach the gospel to the poor; He hath sent Me to heal the broken-hearted, to preach deliverance to the captives, and recovering of sight to the blind, to set at liberty them that are bruised." (Luke 4:18)

Questions:

List 3 benefits of corporate prayer.

_____

_____

_____

How active are you in praying with other believers?

_____

_____

_____

What attitudes should believers have when they pray corporately?

_____

_____

_____

Why do you think God commands a blessing upon unity?

_____

_____

_____

Actively and intentionally pursue to participate in a corporate prayer gathering.

"All of us together can do more than any of us can do alone!"

Lesson 5
Persistent Prayer

Persistence: means to persevere and not to faint. Be steadfast. Be devoted and constant.

"Rejoicing in hope; patient in tribulation; **_continuing instant in prayer_**;" (Romans 12:12)

"**_Pray without ceasing_**." (1 Thessalonians 5:17)

"Elias was a man subject to like passions as we are, and he prayed earnestly that it might not rain: and it rained not on the earth by the space of three years and six months." "And **_he prayed again_**, and the heaven gave rain, and the earth brought forth her fruit." (James 5:17-18)

Many believers misunderstand when it comes to the difference between vain repetitions and persistent praying. In (Matthew 6:7) "But when ye pray, use not vain repetitions, as the heathen [do]: for they think that they shall be heard for their much speaking." Jesus told the hypocritical Pharisees that they won't be heard because of their vain repetitious prayers. Christ was referring to the Pharisees desire to be seen by man for their fancy prayers rather than be heard by God. You and I must always make sure that we are never trying to be impressive when we pray. We should always pray to an audience of one, God our Father!

Elijah is a perfect example of persistent praying. He operated in Prophetic Prayer intercession, which [is] a "Word" from God prayed by revelation into manifestation. (John 5:14) And this is the confidence that we have in him, that, if we ask any thing according to his will, he heareth us: And if we know that he hear us, whatsoever we ask, we know that we have the petitions that we desired of him.

God is only obligated to bring to pass what He has designated!

Persistent Praying should rest on the revelation of Scriptures or what the Spirit has spoken: (Divine Download) "And it came to pass [after] many days, that the word of the LORD came to Elijah in the third year, saying, Go, shew thyself unto Ahab; and I will send rain upon the earth." (1 Kings 18:1)

Persistent Prayer requires a process: Go again seven times. (Divine Discipline) "So Ahab went up to eat and to drink. And Elijah went up to the top of Carmel; and he cast himself down upon the earth, and put his face between his knees, And said to his servant, Go up now, look toward the sea. And he went up, and looked, and said, [There is] nothing. And he said, Go again seven times." (1 Kings 18:42)

Persistent Prayer resists problems: (Divine Determination) "And said to his servant, Go up now, look toward the sea. And he went up, and looked, and said, *[There is] nothing*. And he said, Go again seven times." (1Kings 18:43)

Persistent Prayer requires personal sacrifice: (Dedication) So Ahab went up to eat and to drink. And Elijah went up to the top of Carmel; and he cast himself down upon the earth, and put his face between his knees, And it came to pass at the seventh time, that he said, Behold, there ariseth a little cloud out of the sea, like a man's hand. (1 Kings 18:42, 44)

Those who received breakthroughs by persistent prayer:
Jacob: received power with God- (Genesis 32:24-32)
Hannah: received a child though she was barren- (1 Samuel 1:12-20)
Daniel: received revelation- (Daniel 10:12-14)
Jonah: received deliverance from the great fish- (Jonah 2:1-10)
Hezekiah: received 15 more years of life- (2 Kings 20:1-11)
Church: received freedom for Peter from a death sentence- (Acts 12:5-16)

Paul and Silas: received a breakthrough out of prison- (Acts 16:25:26)

Christ: received strength to endured the cross- (Matthew 26:36-46)

Questions:

Why do you think it's vital that you remain persistent in prayer?

_____

_____

_____

_____

List some things that often distract you from being persistent in prayer?

_____

_____

_____

Recall a time you remained persistent in prayer and write down the results.

_____

_____

_____

List some people and things you want to persist in prayer about. Spend some time praying about them.

_____

_____

_____

_____

Lesson 6
Pattern of Jesus the Intercessor Who Changes Everything

"For [there is] one God, and ***one mediator between God and men, the man Christ Jesus***; Who gave himself a ransom for all, to be testified in due time."
 (1 Timothy 2:5-6)

The Gospel, or Good News, contains not only the message that Jesus died for us to pay our debt of sin to God, but has resurrected and lives to make intercession for us. (Hebrews 7:25) states, Wherefore he is able also to save them to the uttermost that come unto God by him, ***seeing he ever liveth to make intercession for them.*** Jesus is alive and advancing His people by His continued work as a Mediator/Intercessor.

Mediator- *Intercessor, reconciler. One who intervenes between two, in order to restore peace and friendship, or form a compact, or ratifying a covenant.* One who stands in the middle between two people and brings them together.

Christ presently continues His ministry through Intercession.
Therefore He is able also to save to the uttermost (completely, perfectly, finally, and for all time and eternity) those who come to God through Him, since He is always living to make petition to God and intercede with Him and intervene for them. (Hebrews 7:25 AMP)

"Who shall lay anything to the charge of God's elect? [It is] God that justifieth. Who [is] he that condemneth? [It is] ***Christ that died, yea rather, that is risen again, who is even at the right hand of God, who also maketh intercession for us.***" (Romans 8:33-34)

Christ's intercession for us should give us as believers great confidence, because Christ's prayers are always heard by the Father. *"Then they took away the stone [from the place] where the dead was laid. And Jesus lifted up [his] eyes, and said, Father, I thank thee that thou hast heard me."*
(John 11:41)
His intercession keeps us from being separated from His love.
"Who shall separate us from the love of Christ? [shall] tribulation, or distress, or persecution, or famine, or nakedness, or peril, or sword? As it is written, For thy

sake we are killed all the day long; we are accounted as sheep for the slaughter. Nay, in all these things we are more than conquerors through him that loved us. For I am persuaded, that neither death, nor life, nor angels, nor principalities, nor powers, nor things present, nor things to come, Nor height, nor depth, nor any other creature, shall be able to separate us from the love of God, which is in Christ Jesus our Lord." (Romans 8:35-39)

What was Jesus' qualification to be an ideal Mediator? JESUS DID NOT SIN! *"For such an high priest became us, who is **holy**, **harmless**, **undefiled**, **separate** from sinners, and **made higher than the heavens**" (Hebrews 7:26)*

For we have not a high priest which cannot be touched with the feeling of our infirmities; but was in all points tempted like as [we are, yet] without sin. (Hebrews 4:15)

Christ died for us to bring us back into right relationship with God
"But God commendeth his love toward us, in that, while we were yet sinners, Christ died for us. Much more then, being now justified by his blood, we shall be saved from wrath through him. For if, when we were enemies, we were reconciled to God by the death of his Son, much more, being reconciled, we shall be saved by his life. And not only [so], but we also joy in God through our Lord Jesus Christ, by whom we have now received the atonement. (Romans 5:8-11)

For if because of one man's trespass (lapse, offense) death reigned through that one, much more surely will those who receive [God's] overflowing grace (unmerited favor) and the free gift of righteousness [putting them into right standing with Himself] *reign as kings in life through the one Man Jesus Christ (the Messiah, the Anointed One).* (Romans 5:17 AMP)

Christ intercession restores us back to the state of reigning together with Him in heavenly places! "And hath raised [us] up together, and made [us] sit together in heavenly [places] in Christ Jesus:" (Ephesians 2:6)

What Changes Everything is a better Covenant through Christ?
But now hath he obtained a more excellent ministry, by how much also he is the mediator of a better covenant, which was established upon better promises. (Hebrews 8:6)

Who is made, not after the law of a carnal commandment, but after the power of an endless life. (Hebrews 7:16)

1. Perfection of His sacrifice- (Hebrews 10:10)
2. Permanence of the covenant- (Hebrews 7:22-25)
3. Power of the covenant- (Hebrews 8:10-11)

1. <u>**The Intercession of Jesus provides for us forgiveness**</u>
 "My little children, these things write I unto you, that ye sin not. And if any man sin, we have an advocate with the Father, Jesus Christ the righteous: And he is the propitiation for our sins: and not for ours only, but also for the sins of the whole world" (I John 2:1, 2), (See also 1 John 1:9).

2. <u>**The Intercession of Jesus can keep us from sin.**</u>
"But this man, because he continueth ever, hath an unchangeable priesthood. Wherefore he is able also to save them to the uttermost (utterly or completely) that come unto God by him, seeing he ever liveth to make intercession for them" (Hebrews 7:24, 25).

For in that he himself hath suffered being tempted, _**he is able to succor them that are tempted.**_ (Hebrews 2:18)

Now unto Him who is able to keep you from falling, and to present you faultless before the presence of His glory with exceeding joy." (Jude 24)

Christ Examples of intercession:
Woman taken in adultery- (John 8:3-11)
Lazarus- (John 11:40-44)
Peter- (Luke 22:31-32)
Thief on the Cross: (Luke 22:39-43)
The Church- "I pray not that thou shouldest take them out of the world, but that thou shouldest keep them from the evil." (John 17:15)

The Help of the Holy Spirit through intercession.
"In the same way, the Spirit helps us in our weakness. We do not know what we ought to pray, but the Spirit himself intercedes for us with groans that words cannot express. And he who searches our hearts knows the mind of the Spirit, because the Spirit intercedes for the saints in accordance with God's will. The indwelling Holy Spirit, through His superior intimate knowledge, both prays for us and joins us in our praying, infusing His prayers into ours so that we "pray in the Spirit." (Romans 8:26, 27)

Two supernatural things happen here:

1. First, the Holy Spirit tells us what we ought to pray for. Apart from the Spirit's assistance, our prayers are limited by our own reason and intuition. But with the Holy Spirit's help they become informed by Heaven. As we seek the Spirit's help, He will speak to us through His Word, which conveys His mind regarding every matter of principle. Thus, in Spirit-directed prayer we will think God's thoughts after Him. His desires will become our desires, His motives our motives, His ends our ends."

2. The energizing of the Holy Spirit for prayer, infusing tired, even infirm, bodies and elevating the depressed to pray with power and conviction for God's work."

"For it is God which worketh in you both to will and to do of [his] good pleasure." (Philippians 2:13)

We reign with Christ through His intercession
That even though we were dead because of our sins, he gave us life when he raised Christ from the dead. (It is only by God's grace that you have been saved!) For he raised us from the dead along with Christ and seated us with him in the heavenly realms because we are united with Christ Jesus. (Ephesians 2:5, 6 NLT)

Energizes us- gave us new life in Him. (Ephesians 2:5)
Elevates us- raised us up. (Ephesians 2:6)
Enthrones us- (Ephesians 2:6)

Notes

_____

_____

_____

_____

_____

_____

_____

_____

_____

_____

_____

_____

_____

Lesson 7
Positioned For Intercession

"And I sought for a man among them, that should make up the hedge, and stand in the gap before me for the land, that I should not destroy it: but I found none." (Ezekiel 22:30)

Intercede: (palal) to *intervene*, interpose, pray, to mediate. Intreat, supplication.

Paga: (Hebrew) to encounter, meet, reach, entreat, make intercession, light upon, join, to meet (of kindness) fall upon (of hostility), entreat (of request), to strike, touch (of boundary), to make attack, to reach the mark. To light upon a person or a thing, fall in with, hit upon, a person or a thing to go to or meet a person, for the purpose of conversation, consultation, or supplication.

Intervene- go in between to *prevent* or *alter* a course of events.
Gap- breach or broken wall.
Hedge- fence or wall.

God had a hedge around His people. But sin broke down that hedge. Man had become alienated from God. God was looking for some man to stand in the gap. Jesus is the one who came and stood in the gap for us, and has reconciled us to God through the blood of His cross.

Broken hedges gives access to the enemy to destroy us!
(Ecclesiastes 10:8) He that diggeth a pit shall fall into it; and whoso breaketh a hedge, a serpent shall bite him.

Through Intercession we become agents of restoration.
"And [they that shall be] of thee shall build the old waste places: thou shalt raise up the foundations of many generations; and thou shalt be called, The repairer of the breach, The restorer of paths to dwell in." (Isaiah 58:12)

"Prayer enables us to touch God on one hand and the needy world on the other."- Wesley Duewel

Charles Spurgeon- "Whenever God determines to do a great work, He first sets His people to pray."

Five key areas to intercede for a person in:

Relationship- with God, families and themselves.

Mind- which includes mind, will, emotions, imaginations, intellect and decisions)

Body- good health

Spirit- remain true and sensitive to the Spirit of Christ

Finances- prosperity, career, good stewardship practices.

Write an intercessory prayer for 3 individuals in one of these five areas.

Intercessory Prayer #1.

_____

_____

_____

Intercessory Prayer #2.

_____

_____

_____

Intercessory Prayer #3.

_____

_____

_____

7 Strategic Areas to Intercede for:
Families
Government
Economy
Religious
Arts and entertainment
Social and News media
Military

Intercession- intervene. Come between as to prevent or alter a result or course of events. To hit the mark of one discharging a javelin or arrow. To reach, attain, obtain, get, become master of. To happen. To specify, to take a case, as for example to meet one, of he who meets one or presents himself unsought, ordinary, common person.

Attributes of an Intercessor

Comprehension- intimate knowledge of God's will.
"When Jesus heard [that], he said, This sickness is not unto death, but for the glory of God, that the Son of God might be glorified thereby." (John 11:4)

Confidence- I believe God is able.
"These things said he: and after that he saith unto them, Our friend Lazarus sleepeth; but I go, that I may awake him out of sleep." (John 11:11)

"Jesus said unto her, I am the resurrection, and the life: he that believeth in me, though he were dead, yet shall he live: And whosoever liveth and believeth in me shall never die. Believest thou this?" (John 11:25-26)

Compassion- touched with the feeling of the pain of others.
"Jesus wept." (John 11:35)

Command- authority in prayer beyond the circumstance.
"Then they took away the stone [from the place] where the dead was laid. And Jesus lifted up [his] eyes, and said, Father, I thank thee that thou hast heard me." (John 11:41)

"And when he thus had spoken, he cried with a loud voice, Lazarus, come forth." (John 11:43)

Completion- loose him and let him go:
"And he that was dead came forth, bound hand and foot with grave clothes: and his face was bound about with a napkin. Jesus saith unto them, Loose him, and let him go." (John 11:44)

Here's an example of how your intercession time could go:
• Spend a few moments praising God for Who He is.
• Pray in tongues to charge your spirit and create sensitivity to the Spirit.

- Make sure you repent of any sin that will hinder your prayer.
- Begin to pray for specific areas from your prayer list.
- Pray according to God's Word concerning the areas you have listed.
- Pray for the desired result God wants to see concerning your subject and pray against anything that will hinder His desired intent.

Example #1

"Father I pray that every husband will love his wife as Christ love the church." In Jesus name!

"Father I bind every evil spirit that influences every husband to be selfish and inattentive to his wife's needs." In Jesus name!

Example #2

"Father I pray that every government leader will lead in righteousness." In Jesus name!

"Father I pray that You would remove every unjust leader." In Jesus name!

Write 2 intercessory prayers based on the 7 strategic areas of intercession that was given. i.e: families, government, economy, etc.

Prayer #1.

_____

_____

_____

_____

_____

_____

_____

Prayer #2.

_____

_____

_____

_____

_____

_____

Lesson 8
Pleasure of Prayer- Joyful in the House of Prayer

"Even them will ***I bring to my holy mountain***, and ***make them joyful in my house of prayer***: their burnt offerings and ***their sacrifices [shall be] accepted*** upon mine altar; for mine house shall be called an house of prayer for all people."
(Isaiah 56:7)

"And said unto them, It is written, My house shall be called the house of prayer; but ye have made it a den of thieves." (Matthew 21:13)

Introduction: I am convinced more believers would pray if they understood the abundance of joy that is released when we pray individually and corporately. When we understand this, Believers will no longer be AWOL from prayer gatherings or neglect their personal prayer times.

"Thou wilt shew me the path of life: in thy presence [is] fullness of joy; at thy right hand [there are] pleasures for evermore." (Psalms 16:11)

Joyful: (Hebrew word is: "samach") to rejoice, made glad, merry. Joy is a supernatural grace received by faith from the Spirit of God that causes a believer to remain in a worshipful, peaceful state in challenging times with an expectation of receiving God's best in every situation.

(Isaiah 56:7) reveals to us the blessing of prayer:
Assistance- I will bring them
Amuse- make them joyful
Acceptance- accept their sacrifice
Acknowledgement- mine house shall be called an house of prayer

"Let all those that seek thee rejoice and be glad in thee: let such as love thy salvation say continually, The LORD be magnified." (Psalms 40:16)

"Glory ye in his holy name: let the heart of them rejoice that seek the LORD." (Psalms 105:3)

"[There is] a river, the streams whereof shall make glad the city of God, the holy [place] of the tabernacles of the most High." (Psalms 46:4)

"And in that day ye shall ask me nothing. Verily, verily, I say unto you, Whatsoever ye shall ask the Father in my name, he will give [it] you. Hitherto have ye asked nothing in my name: ask, and ye shall receive, that your joy may be full." (John 16:23-24)

"For the kingdom of God is not meat and drink; but righteousness, and peace, and joy in the Holy Ghost." (Romans 14:17)

God rejoices over His people.
(Zephaniah 3:17) "The LORD thy God in the midst of thee [is] mighty; he will save, he will rejoice over thee with joy; he will rest in his love, he will joy over thee with singing."

Examples of those who were made joyful in prayer:
Hannah: "And Hannah prayed, and said, My heart rejoiceth in the LORD, mine horn is exalted in the LORD: my mouth is enlarged over mine enemies; because I rejoice in thy salvation." (1 Samuel 2:1)

Jehoshaphat: "Then they returned, every man of Judah and Jerusalem, and Jehoshaphat in the forefront of them, to go again to Jerusalem with joy; for the LORD had made them to rejoice over their enemies." (2 Chronicles 20:27)

Paul and Silas: "And at midnight Paul and Silas prayed, and sang praises unto God: and the prisoners heard them." (Acts 16:25)

Questions:

Why is joy such a benefit to a believer?

_____

_____

_____

Can you remember a time when God poured out His joy upon a corporate prayer gathering? How did it make you feel? What was the fellowship like among the group?

_____

_____

_____

_____

What can you do to maintain a joyful attitude in prayer?

_____

_____

_____

_____

Lesson 9
Patterns of Prayer

"Praying always with all prayer and supplication in the Spirit, and watching thereunto with all perseverance and supplication for all saints;" (Ephesians 6:18)

Prayer is an **intentional** communion with God that builds an **intimate** relationship with the Father and releases Him to get **involved** in human affairs. Prayer brings us into partnership and agreement with the Lord for the fulfillment of His purpose in the earth.

E. M. Bounds on Prayer said that prayer is the umbilical cord of God in which Christians receive their nourishment for a healthy spiritual life in God."

Prayer is the love language of God: "The sacrifice of the wicked [is] an abomination to the LORD: but the prayer of the upright [is] his delight."
(Proverbs 15:8)

1. **Praying always-** constantly prayer about all things

2. **Pray always with all prayer: types of prayers-** Adoration, Thanksgiving, Supplication, Petition, Intercession.

3. **Supplication**: (Greek: deēsis or de-a-sis) need, want, a seeking, asking, entreating for favor

Prayers: (Greek: proseuchē or Pros-yu-kha) earnest prayer manifesting seriousness and sincerity.

Intercessions: (Greek: enteuxis or en-tyu-kses) meeting with, petition, to make attack to reach the mark.

Giving of thanks or thanksgiving: (Greek: eucharistia) gratitude and appreciation.

4. **Pray in the Spirit-** praying with the Holy Spirits assistance.

5. **Watching and Prayer.** "Jesus told His disciples to watch and pray lest they enter into temptation." (Matthew 26:41)

This type of watchfulness in prayer means remaining alert against the enemy's attack (1 Peter 5:8) and it also means having a sense of expectancy for what God promises to do. Elijah was praying for rain on Mt. Carmel and kept sending his servant to look for a cloud in the Western sky, he was in a sense watching and praying. He was waiting for and expecting an answer to his prayer.

6. **Prayer is perseverance: That is pressing on until the answer comes.**
"For God is my witness, whom I serve with my spirit in the gospel of his Son, that without ceasing I make mention of you always in my prayers;" (Romans 1:9)

"Pray without ceasing." (1 Thessalonians 5:17)

"Rejoicing in hope; patient in tribulation; continuing instant in prayer;" (Romans 12:12)

Jacobs Example of perseverance.

"And Jacob was left alone; and there wrestled a man with him until the breaking of the day. And when he saw that of Jacob's thigh was out of joint, as he wrestled with him. And he said, Let me go, for the day breaketh. And he said, I will not let thee go, except thou bless me. And he said unto him, What [is] thy name? And he said, Jacob. And he said, Thy name shall be called no more Jacob, but Israel: for as a prince hast thou power with God and with men, and hast prevailed. And Jacob asked [him], and said, Tell [me], I pray thee, thy name. And he said, Wherefore [is] it [that] thou dost ask after my name? And he blessed him there. And Jacob called the name of the place Peniel: for I have seen God face to face, and my life is preserved." (Genesis 32:24-30)

Who are we to pray for? "All saints."

Samuel said it's a sin not to pray for one another.
"Moreover as for me, God forbid that I should sin against the LORD in ceasing to pray for you: but I will teach you the good and the right way:" (1 Samuel 12:23)

Abraham interceded for Lot and the city of Sodom. (Genesis 18:17-33)
Moses interceding for the people of Israel. (Exodus 17:11, Numbers 11:2)
Daniel for Israel: (Daniel 9:3-21)
Nehemiah for Jerusalem: (Nehemiah 1:4-11)
Jesus Prayed for Peter- (Luke 22:31, 1 Peter 5:8)
Church Prayed for Peter- (Acts 12:5)

Paul prayed always for the saints.
"For God is my witness, whom I serve with my spirit in the gospel of his Son, that without ceasing I make mention of you always in my prayers;" (Romans 1:9)

"I thank God, whom I serve from [my] forefathers with pure conscience, that without ceasing I have remembrance of thee in my prayers night and day;"
(2 Timothy 1:3)

The Blessing of praying for others.
"And the LORD turned the captivity of Job, when he prayed for his friends: also the LORD gave Job twice as much as he had before." (Job 42:10)

Pray that God will fill them with the knowledge of His will.
"For this cause we also, since the day we heard [it], do not cease to pray for you, and to desire that ye might be filled with the knowledge of his will in all wisdom and spiritual understanding; That ye might walk worthy of the Lord unto all pleasing, being fruitful in every good work, and increasing in the knowledge of

<u>God; Strengthened with all might, according to his glorious power, unto all patience and longsuffering with joyfulness; (Colossians 1:9-11)</u>

Because of this, since the day we heard about you, we have continued praying for you, asking God that you will know fully what he wants. We pray that you will also have great <u>wisdom and understanding in spiritual things</u> so that you <u>will live the kind of life that honors and pleases the Lord in every way. You will produce fruit in every good work and grow in the knowledge of God. God will strengthen you with his own great power so that you will not give up when troubles come, but you will be patient. And you will joyfully</u> give thanks to the Father who has made you able to have a share in all that he has prepared for his people in the kingdom of light. (Colossians 1:9-12 NCV)

Pray for their healing: "Confess [your] faults one to another, and pray one for another, that ye may be healed. The effectual fervent prayer of a righteous man availeth much." (James 5:16)

Pray for all men: I exhort therefore, that, first of all, supplications, prayers, intercessions, [and] giving of thanks, be made for all men; For kings, and [for] all that are in authority; that we may lead a quiet and peaceable life in all godliness and honesty. For this [is] good and acceptable in the sight of God our Saviour; Who will have all men to be saved, and to come unto the knowledge of the truth." (1 Timothy 2:1-4)

Pray for their spiritual enlightenment.
"Cease not to give thanks for you, making mention of you in my prayers; That the God of our Lord Jesus Christ, the Father of glory, may give unto you the spirit of wisdom and revelation in the knowledge of him: The eyes of your understanding being enlightened; that ye may know what is the hope of his calling, and what the riches of the glory of his inheritance in the saints." (Ephesians 1:16-18)

Lesson 10
Power of Partnership with the Holy Spirit in Prayer

It is crucial that we learn how to partner with the Holy Spirit in prayer. One of the Holy Spirit's assignment is to aid believers in fulfilling the purposes of God on the earth through prayer. "Without the Spirit we can't, without us He won't!" We must exercise the daily discipline of yielding to the directives of the Spirit in prayer. We must reverence and respect His precious presence in our lives.

*The Spirit of God gives you and I power for effectiveness in prayer. The Greek word for **power is "dynamis"** which means strength, ability, and power for performing miracles. It's the Holy Spirit that causes miracle working power to be released through our prayers.*

(Acts 1:8) But ye shall receive power, after that the Holy Ghost is come upon you: and ye shall be witnesses unto me both in Jerusalem, and in all Judaea, and in Samaria, and unto the uttermost part of the earth.

Jesus was able to pray with power because of the anointing of the Holy Spirit.
(Acts 10:38) "How God anointed Jesus of Nazareth with the Holy Ghost and with power: who went about doing good, and healing all that were oppressed of the devil; for God was with him.

The Holy Spirit gives us power to pray. Through Spirit empowered praying we can bind up brokenness, loose captives and open spiritual prisons freeing those whom the enemy has taken captive at will.

Notice the power in Jesus praying for the resurrection of Lazarus.
(John 11:41-44) Then they took away the stone [from the place] where the dead was laid. And Jesus lifted up [his] eyes, and said, Father, I thank thee that thou hast heard me. And I knew that thou hearest me always: but because of the people which stand by I said [it], that they may believe that thou hast sent me. And when he thus had spoken, he cried with a loud voice, Lazarus, come forth. And he that was dead came forth, bound hand and foot with graveclothes: and his face was bound about with a napkin. Jesus saith unto them, Loose him, and let him go.

(Romans 8:14) For as many as are led by the Spirit of God, they are the sons of God. **The word "led" means to be prompted, guided, directed, to lead by laying hold of, to bring to the point of destination. As we allow the Spirit to guide us in prayer, He will reveal strategic keys; give guidance and directives that will yield tremendous results in our praying. He will give us an inward witness on what and how to pray.**
(Romans 8:16) The Spirit itself beareth witness with our spirit.....

In (2 Corinthians 2), Paul states that the Spirit of God makes known to us the deep things of God. He gives us great advantage by helping us to know the deep things of God when we pray.

(1 Corinthians 2:10) But God hath revealed [them] unto us by his Spirit: for the Spirit searcheth all things, yea, the deep things of God.

(1 Corinthians 2:12) Now we have received, not the spirit of the world, but the spirit which is of God; that we might know the things that are freely given to us of God.

(1 Corinthians 2:14) But the natural man receiveth not the things of the Spirit of God: for they are foolishness unto him: neither can he know [them], because they are spiritually discerned.

He guides our praying so that we are praying according to God's truth about a situation. He speaks the plans of God so that our praying is in concert with what the Father wills. He also show us things to come by giving us a word, dreams images, pictures or visions so are praying is in tune with God's plan. (John 16:13) Howbeit when he, the Spirit of truth, is come, he will guide you into all truth: for he shall not speak of himself; but whatsoever he shall hear, [that] shall he speak: and he will shew you things to come.

Testimony: I remember once being very distraught about ministry and was ready to give it up. The Spirit of God spoke to me in a dream that my harvest was coming in the winter. He said, through all the hard and cold things you have been through, I'm going to make you fruitful. He told me in no uncertain terms, "Get Back to your Future!" Had I not had that dream I would have forsaken the truth of what God had planned and would have given in to the enemy's lie. Needless to say I got back to my future and started praying according to what the Spirit of God had revealed to me. In the winter of 2005 God enabled our congregation to purchase not one, but two facilitates to house our vision. Thank God for the Ministry of His wonderful Spirit to me that speaks and shows us things to come!

(Acts 2:17) And it shall come to pass in the last days, saith God, I will pour out of my Spirit upon all flesh: and your sons and your daughters shall prophesy, and your young men shall see visions, and your old men shall dream dreams:

Paul sought the Lord three times for relief from the enemy's attack. The Spirit of God answered his prayers by giving him the necessary revelation for breakthrough. (2 Corinthians 12:8-10) For this thing I besought the Lord thrice, that it might depart from me. And he said unto me, My grace is sufficient for thee: for my strength is made perfect in weakness. Most gladly therefore will I rather glory in my infirmities, that the power of Christ may rest upon me. Therefore I take pleasure in infirmities, in reproaches, in necessities, in persecutions, in distresses for Christ's sake: for when I am weak, then am I strong.

Ananias received direction from the Spirit of the Lord to pray for Paul.
(Acts 9:10-12) And there was a certain disciple at Damascus, named Ananias; and to him said the Lord in a vision, Ananias. And he said, Behold, I [am here], Lord. And the Lord [said] unto him, Arise, and go into the street which is called Straight, and enquire in the house of Judas for [one] called Saul, of Tarsus: for, behold, he prayeth, And hath seen in a vision a man named Ananias coming in, and putting [his] hand on him, that he might receive his sight.

(Acts 9:17-18) And Ananias went his way, and entered into the house; and putting his hands on him said, Brother Saul, the Lord, [even] Jesus, that appeared unto thee in the way as thou camest, hath sent me, that thou mightest receive thy sight, and be filled with the Holy Ghost. And immediately there fell from his eyes as it had been scales: and he received sight forthwith, and arose, and was baptized.

When the Spirit of God resides in and upon a believer, He makes available a variety of gifts to help us get the job done in prayer. You must learn to flow with the Spirit by faith so that He can activate these graces when needed.

(1 Corinthians 12:7-10) But the manifestation of the Spirit is given to every man to profit withal. For to one is given by the Spirit the word of wisdom; to another the word of knowledge by the same Spirit; To another faith by the same Spirit; to another the gifts of healing by the same Spirit; To another the working of miracles; to another prophecy; to another discerning of spirits; to another [divers] kinds of tongues; to another the interpretation of tongues:

Testimony of how the Holy Spirit helps us in prayer through gifts: Once I encountered a woman in my church who was demon possessed. After a time in prayer concerning the situation with a dear friend in the Lord. The Spirit of God gave a Word of Knowledge to my friend what type of demon it was and how it had come through the family line by a relative who had practice witchcraft. Through the Holy Spirit's revelation and directives we were able to help this woman get free from the enemy.

When threaten the Apostles knew exactly what to pray to experience greater power and continue ministry momentum. The Holy Spirit in prayer will charge our words of prayer with life giving, transformative power to change current negative conditions. (Acts 4:31-35) And when they had prayed, the place was shaken where they were assembled together; and they were all filled with the Holy Ghost, and they spake the word of God with boldness. And the multitude of them that believed were of one heart and of one soul: neither said any [of them] that ought of the things which he possessed was his own; but they had all things common. And with great power gave the apostles witness of the resurrection of the Lord Jesus: and great grace was upon them all. Neither was there any among them that lacked: for as many as were possessors of lands or houses sold them, and brought the prices of the things that were sold, And laid [them] down at the apostles' feet: and distribution was made unto every man according as he had need.

Paul's Spirit-led prayers for the church in Ephesus caused them to experience supernatural growth and advancement. (Ephesians 1:16-19) Cease not to give thanks for you, making mention of you in my prayers; That the God of our Lord Jesus Christ, the Father of glory, may give unto you the spirit of wisdom and revelation in the knowledge of him: The eyes of your understanding being enlightened; that ye may know what is the hope of his calling, and what the riches of the glory of his inheritance in the saints, And what [is] the exceeding greatness of his power to us-ward who believe, according to the working of his mighty power.

The Spirit of God cause life giving rivers to flow from our inner most being, releasing transformation and causing believers to bless the lives of others through the ministry of prayer. (John 7:38) He that believeth on me, as the scripture hath said, out of his belly shall flow rivers of living water.

(Psalms 104:30) Thou sendest forth thy spirit, they are created: and thou renewest the face of the earth.

The Holy Spirit helps us in prayer to overcome physical and spiritual limitations in prayer, downloading to us the mind of God. (Romans 8:26-27) Likewise the Spirit also helpeth our infirmities: for we know not what we should pray for as we ought: but the Spirit itself maketh intercession for us with groanings which cannot be uttered. And he that searcheth the hearts knoweth what [is] the mind of the Spirit, because he maketh intercession for the saints according to [the will of] God.

Testimony: There was a time in my life when I was diagnosed with Ulcerative Colitis which is an inflammatory bowel disease. The Spirit of God led me to a book by Kenneth Hagin titled Healing Scriptures. I remember praying and confessing (Ephesians 5:30) "For we are members of his body, of his flesh, and of his bones." The Spirit of God illuminated this verse to me and reveals that I am a member of Christ's body. He revealed to me that Jesus never experienced being sick or was ever diseased in His body. Therefore if I'm a part of His body and of His flesh and bones, if there was no sickness in His body, sickness and disease must leave my body. For what's in Christ (healing), is in me, therefore I am healed. Immediately Ulcerative Colitis ceased controlling my life! I was and am healed!

Keys to staying connected to the Spirit in prayer:

1. Live a holy life: (1 Corinthians 6:20) For ye are bought with a price: therefore glorify God in your body, and in your spirit, which are God's.

2. Read and meditate on the Word of God: (Psalms 1:2-3) But his delight [is] in the law of the LORD; and in his law doth he meditate day and night. And he shall be like a tree planted by the rivers of water, that bringeth forth his fruit in his season; his leaf also shall not wither; and whatsoever he doeth shall prosper.

3. Live a lifestyle of faith: (Hebrews 11:6) But without faith [it is] impossible to please [him]: for he that cometh to God must believe that he is, and [that] he is a rewarder of them that diligently seek him.

4. Set aside time for worship: (Psalms 22:3) But thou [art] holy, [O thou] that inhabitest the praises of Israel.

5. Spend time in prayer: (1 Thessalonians 5:17) Pray without ceasing.
(Jude 1:20) But ye, beloved, building up yourselves on your most holy faith, praying in the Holy Ghost,

Activation:

Spend some time in fellowship with the Holy Spirit in prayer. Praying in tongues help build you spiritually to receive from the Holy Spirit.

(1 Corinthians 14:2-3) For he that speaketh in an [unknown] tongue speaketh not unto men, but unto God: for no man understandeth [him]; howbeit in the spirit he speaketh mysteries. But he that prophesieth speaketh unto men [to] edification, and exhortation, and comfort.

While praying ask the Holy Spirit to show you things He desires for you to pray.

Be sensitive to images, words, dreams or visions the Holy Spirit give to you to pray about.

Spend time prayerfully in the Word being careful of revelation the Spirit gives to you to pray.

Write down things you are receiving from the Holy Spirit and take some time to pray about them.

Lesson 11

Prayer Vocabulary

"How forcible are right words!" (Job 6:25)

Arrest- bring under subjection and cause to cease.

Abort- terminate

Bind- to prohibit undesirable spiritual activities

Declare- to state authoritatively. An announcement which results in a court action.

Decree- is an official order, edict, or decision enforced by law. In our kingdom role we must accept our God-given jurisdictional authority and effectively utilize our power through the spoken word.

Employ- to utilize the service or assistance of another

Forbid- to refuse to allow

Limitations- anything that restricts, constrains or confine

Loose- release or emancipate from an assignment

Obliterate- destroy completely

Overthrow- to cause destruction and downfall

Rebuke- censure, denounce

Resist- defiantly withstand

Stirring- action to elicit or release a response or activity.

Strongman- high ranking principality assigned as a gatekeeper to a person, people or a region.

Superimpose- place on top of, overruling

Lesson 12

Promises of Answered Prayer

(Psalms 65:2) "O thou that hearest prayer, unto thee shall all flesh come."

(Job 22:27) "Thou shalt make thy prayer unto him, and he shall hear thee, and thou shalt pay thy vows."

(Psalms 6:9) "The LORD hath heard my supplication; the LORD will receive my prayer."

(Psalms 66:20) "Blessed [be] God, which hath not turned away my prayer, nor his mercy from me."

(Psalms 102:17) "He will regard the prayer of the destitute, and not despise their prayer."

(Proverbs 15:8) "The sacrifice of the wicked [is] an abomination to the LORD: but the prayer of the upright [is] his delight."

(Proverbs 15:29) "The LORD [is] far from the wicked: but he heareth the prayer of the righteous."

(Matthew 21:22) "And all things, whatsoever ye shall ask in prayer, believing, ye shall receive."

(James 5:16) "Confess [your] faults one to another, and pray one for another, that ye may be healed. The effectual fervent prayer of a righteous man availeth much."

(Deuteronomy 4:7) "For what nation [is there so] great, who [hath] God [so] nigh unto them, as the LORD our God [is] in all [things that] we call upon him [for]?"

(Psalms 50:15) "And call upon me in the day of trouble: I will deliver thee, and thou shalt glorify me."

(Isaiah 55:6) "Seek ye the LORD while he may be found, call ye upon him while he is near:"

(Jeremiah 33:3) "Call unto me, and I will answer thee, and shew thee great and mighty things, which thou knowest not."

Final Word

My prayer is that the principles, patterns and practices in this book will bless your life as it has blessed mine. For me prayer is not just a practice in life but it is my life. Prayer is the most precious and enjoyable disciplines of my life. The greatest reward to me regarding prayer is the privilege and pleasure of communing with my Heavenly Father.

I was raised as a young man without a father. My father had died when I was an infant. I remember in my times of growing up wishing I had a father like the other young boys in my neighborhood. I longed for a Father's love, instruction and even correction.

When I became a born again Christian I soon began to understand that I was never without a father. My Heavenly Father was always there directing, correcting and navigating me into the course of life that He had planned for me. As I began to mature in Christ, I had this insatiable desire to spend hours in the presence of God. I would stay up late in the wee hours of the morning talking with God and learning His Word. I would wake up eager to share what He had shown me with others.

I have been a Christian now for over 30 years and my passion for the presence of God and His Word are still at a feverishly high level. I have received so much joy and pleasure in His presence, it's my desire to bring everyone that I possibly can into an intimate and life changing relationship with Christ.

I use to think that I was the one wooing Him, but I soon discovered that He was wooing me all the time. I strongly believe that Christ is wooing you my friend, this is the reason you are studying from this book. Consider yourself wooed!

Notes

_____

_____

_____

_____

_____

_____

_____

_____

_____

_____

_____

_____

_____

_____

About the Author

Apostle David A. Davis received his calling while serving in the U.S. Army in Fayetteville, North Carolina at Ft. Bragg. Upon being transferred to the Republic of Panama, he established a Pentecostal worship service for soldiers and the local citizens in the Panama Canal Zone where he shared a successful pastorate alongside his lovely wife Sharon for more than two years. God used Apostle Davis and his wife to bring hope, help and helping to the region. Apostle Davis is a prolific preacher who operates in the ministry of deliverance as well as in the prophetic.

Apostle Davis serves presently as the Founder and Senior Leader of the Greater Life Church in Lakewood, Washington along with his dynamic help mate Pastor Sharon Davis. Under their anointed leadership, the members of Greater Life Church are being upgraded to carry out their ministry assignments in excellence and the Church has grown wonderfully. Apostle Davis and his wife, Pastor Sharon have made several televised appearances on Trinity Broadcasting Network-Seattle and have a standing engagement to host the show.

Apostle Davis has a passion to empower believers to reach their full potential, overturn strongholds and deliver nations to God. He leads a weekly prayer call which consists of people from all over the U.S.

Apostle Davis is known as "Fireball" for his passionate and fiery teachings, preaching and prayers!

Power of Prayer

Greater Life Ministries
Touching Hearts, Teaching Truth, Transforming Lives

Sunday
9:30 a.m.   Hour of Power Service
11:30 a.m.   Worship Service

Monday
6:56 a.m.   Strike Force Prayer Call (559) 726-1300 Code 979541#
7:00 p.m.   Women's Mentorship (13 years and up)

Tuesday
7:00 p.m.   Men's Mentorship (13 years and up)

Wednesday
6:00 p.m.   Corporate Prayer Training
7:00 p.m.   Biblical Training

Please visit with us on http://www.thegreaterlifechurch.com

Greater Life Church
8222 Washington Blvd SW
Lakewood, WA 98498
(253) 581-4478
Glc_support@comcast.net